RESOURCE CENTRE
WESTERN ISLES LIBRARIES

Readers are requested to take great care of the item while in their possession, and to point out any defects that they may notice in them to the Librarian.
This item should be returned on or before the latest date stamped below, but an extension of the period of loan may be granted when desired.

DATE OF RETURN	DATE OF RETURN	DATE OF RETURN
. . . .	. . . .	. . . .
. . . .	. . . .	. . . .
. . . .	. . . .	. . . .
. . . .	. . . .	. . . .
. . . .	. . . .	. . . .
. . . .	. . . .	. . . .
. . . .	. . . .	. . . .
. . . .	. . . .	. . . .
. . . .	. . . .	. . . .
. . . .	. . . .	. . . .
. . . .	. . . .	. . . .
. . . .	. . . .	. . . .

A mink, a fink, a Skating rink

What is a Noun?

by Brian P. Cleary

illustrated by Jenya Prosmitsky

BOOK 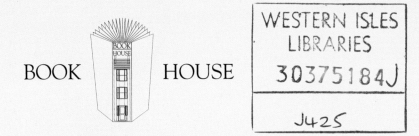 HOUSE

Hill
is a
noun.

Mill
is a
noun.

Gown
is a
noun.

Crown is a noun.

In fact,
our whole
town is
a noun.

If it's a deck,
a duck,
or deer,

If it's
a crystal
chandelier,

If it's a train,

or brain,
or frown,

It's elementary -
it's a noun.

Nouns can sometimes be quite proper,

Like London Bridge, or Edward Hopper,

Big Ben,

Levis,

pekingese-

Proper nouns
name all of these.

A jail,
a nail,

a bale
of hay,
The pool or park in
which you play,

A pound, a hound, a pencil, or pear –

Nouns can be seen everywhere.

A box,
a lip,
a chocolate
chip,

A cup or glass

from which you sip,

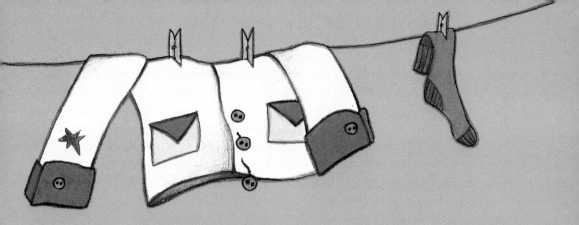

A pocket, button,
sleeve or cuff –

A noun can simply
be your stuff.

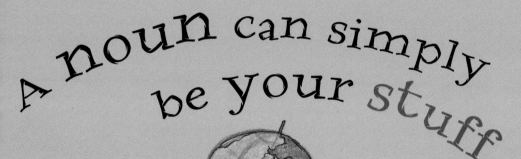

A mink, a fink, a skating rink,

A cake, a rake, your kitchen sink,

The pope,
some soap

that's on a rope,
A downtown shop,
a downhill
slope.

A house
a mouse,
a broken
clock,

New Mexico,

an old
white
sock,

Some tar,
a bar,

a baseball
star,

The place where
mother
parks
her car.

RESERVED for MoM

A noun
can be your
Auntie
Lynn,

The mayor
of the town
You're in,

Your friend
who tells
you awful
jokes –

A noun can be your
favourite folks.

A collar,
a scholar,
a handful
of sand,

Saxes and
faxes, the brass
in the band,

A cat,
a bat,
your
grandma's
hat–

Nouns are a little
of this and that.

If it's a place of any kind –

9

A mountain, hall, or road number 9,

If it's a **country**, county, or town,

Then surely, Shirley, it's a noun.

A king,
a queen,
some
gasoline,

A red
raspberry
ice machine.

If it's a person, place, or thing—

Your dad, the zoo, a diamond ring,

LIONS
TIGERS
BEARS

So, what is a noun? Do you know?

AUTHOR: BRIAN P. CLEARY is the author of several other books for children, including *To root, to toot, to parachute: What is a Verb?*

ILLUSTRATOR: JENYA PROSMITSKY grew up and studied art in Kishinev, Moldova, and now lives in Minneapolis in the USA. Her two cats, Henry and Freddy, were vital to her illustrations for this book.

To Molly, Matt, and Andy — three very proper nouns — B.P.C.

To my mum, who has always been crazy about cats, and my dad, who surprised me by bringing home a kitten when I was 10 — J.P.

Published in Great Britain in 2003 by
Book House, an imprint of
The Salariya Book Company Ltd
25 Marlborough Place, Brighton BN1 1UB

Please visit the Salariya Book Company at:
www.salariya.com
www.book-house.co.uk

ISBN 1 904194 64 8

A catalogue record for this book is available from the British Library.

Printed and bound in USA.